# FIX THEM
## OR
# FIRE THEM

*Managing, Evaluating and
Terminating Underperforming
Employees*

D0916072

## Steven J. Shaer

ISBN: 0615872808
ISBN 13: 978-0615872803
Library of Congress Control Number: 2013948779

# About the Author

Steven Shaer has an eclectic background that spans entrepreneurship, corporate management, and management consulting. He has an undergraduate degree in computer science from Rensselaer Polytechnic Institute and a Master of Business Administration from New York University. In his early career, he was a manager and technologist for IBM, Deloitte, and Accenture. As an entrepreneur, he was instrumental in founding and leading several companies in industries as diverse as technology services, distribution, security technology, and international resort development. In 2000, *Inc.* magazine named a company that Steven founded and was the president of as the thirty-eighth fastest-growing company in America.

In 2007, he founded Shaer and Associates (http://www.shaer-associates.com), which provides consulting, coaching, and training. His areas of specialty include marketing and sales, leadership development, and executive coaching.

Steven is the author of numerous articles and of the book *The Lawyer's Guide to Building Your Practice with Referrals*, which the American Bar Association published in 2013.

# Acknowledgments

I am amazed that anyone can complete a book, however brief, without significant help from friends and associates. While the ideas put forth in this book are ideas that have come from my experiences as a manager, entrepreneur, consultant, and coach, I have also had a team of mentors, coaches, and idea sounding boards who were at least as important. Among them, Jim Muehlhausen, Joseph Patton, and Merrick Leigh were very generous with their time in helping me with the idea development, book structure, and editing. I am grateful to attorneys John C. Malloy III and Meredith Frank Mendez of the Miami law firm Malloy & Malloy, P.L. who provided valuable legal insight to the project.

# Contents

# Introduction

Far too often, managers are reluctant to fire underperforming employees and, as a result, company performance levels suffer. There is no question that firing an employee is one of the more traumatic and emotionally difficult things a manager can do, and as a result, it is something managers often procrastinate doing.

A long time ago, a mentor gave me this advice:

> "You hire based on skills, you fire based on attitude.…When was the last time you fired someone with weak skills but a great attitude? When you hire, why do you focus so much on a candidate's skills on their résumé?"

The reality is, *we almost never fire someone who is a hard worker with a great attitude.* If people are hard workers with great attitudes, we tend to work with them to try to find a place in our organizations where their skills can apply, or we are much more willing to invest in their training to help them get the skills they need to find a home in our company. It is ironic that when we hire, we are keenly focused on the skills someone brings to the table when what we are really looking for is a *great attitude and the ability to learn.* We are ready, willing, and able to invest in those people.

Another mentor gave me this advice:

> "Fire quickly and hire slowly. You will never say that you wish you kept an employee you fired...but you *will* say that you wish you fired them sooner."

Has a manager ever regretted firing someone for performance reasons after the fact? I doubt it. I doubt that managers say, "I wish I kept Bob around for a few months even though he was an underperformer. I think we should have waited until September before we fired him." I am sure you will agree that almost every single time, mangers will say, "I wish I had fired Bob sooner. Things are so much better now that we have someone in his position making more of a contribution."

I have used the lessons in this book as a manager, executive coach, and trainer. Working with clients, I have developed the script for firing employees presented in Chapter 5 and have taught it to a number of executives who have used it with great success. One of my clients asked me to teach a course on using the script (which is called the "Shaer Script" internally) at his company's management retreat.

That client believed his company was holding on to people too long who had below-acceptable performance. He believed that too many employees were in a purgatory state between acceptable performance and performance that was bad enough to warrant firing them, and they remained there way too long hurting overall company performance and esprit de corps. The organization was having difficulty creating and sticking to what I call an "Absolute Binary Performance Plan"—a ninety-day performance plan for underperforming employees that has only two outcomes: acceptable performance or termination. I knew I needed to expand the material to explore managing the underperforming employee. I developed this book from the material I prepared for that management retreat.

I wrote this book from the perspective of a manager at a company with one hundred or more employees. These tend to be companies with more formal human resource policies and management structures. The lessons are just as good for entrepreneurs and smaller company managers, but they probably need to be adapted a bit to these less formal environments. Structured management policies are something that smaller enterprises can learn from larger companies. These policies are valuable in enhancing management communication and performance change, as well as in reducing lawsuit liability, the potential for bad press, and business disruption when employees are fired.

This book and its methods have not been vetted by legal counsel. I strongly recommend that all human resource and management policies be reviewed and approved by competent legal counsel.

# Chapter 1

# To Fire or Fix an Employee

To fire someone or not fire someone—is that the question? In today's litigious world of strict human resource policies and procedure manuals, the question is really whether or not we put underperforming employees on what I call an "Absolute Binary Performance Plan"—a ninety-day performance improvement plan that, in an either–or fashion, fixes their performance or leads directly to their termination. The alternative is that we choose to do nothing definitive about underperforming employees and keep them on at an underperforming level. Too often, managers avoid the confrontation and procedural and legal hassles of an employee termination. They hope for the best and, in doings so, create an environment in which there is no real threat of employee termination. The Absolute Binary Performance Plan is discussed at length in Chapter 3.

It is a sad reality today that many managers perceive the hassles of firing someone as not being worth their career risk. Too much can go wrong. Wrongful-dismissal lawsuits are rampant, and the last thing managers want to have happen is that *their* performance in an employee's firing process gets elevated to the attention of senior management. This situation is compounded when the employee could have a discrimination claim based on his or her status as a member of a preferred group.

Economically, it is important to remember that it is far more efficient for your company and you to transform underperforming employees into satisfactorily performing employees than it is to fire them or even to accept their level of underperformance. Hiring and training a new employee is a lot more expensive and time-consuming than counseling an existing employee to get his or her performance up to par. It may take months to hire and train a new employee, and then you don't know for sure that he or she will be a better performer than the employee you just fired!

Imagine firing an employee; going through the effort and time of interviewing and hiring a new employee; then on-boarding, training, and mentoring him or her. With much of that work, falling on you, the manager and after all of that, you then face the risk that the new employee might not perform well, in which case you will have to do it all over again. It could take months before your team reaches the productivity level you need. This risk is often daunting for many managers, and it can paralyze them from acting. Fixing an employee's performance should be your first priority—it is a lot easier and less risky than termination. Not only will you have an employee who is performing at an acceptable level; you will have an employee whose strengths and weaknesses you will know. There will be few or no surprises. Firing someone is the last resort but often a necessary one. The sooner you determine that an employee can't be "fixed" effectively, the sooner you will be able to bring in someone who *can* perform.

I often find that when my clients are faced with all of the work associated with firing, hiring a replacement, training that new employee, and dealing with the inefficiency of the new person until he or she gets up to speed, they are simply overwhelmed with the process. It is an overwhelming addition to their already busy days. This is a key factor in managers' tendency to procrastinate—not just about firing someone but about doing the work necessary to address the behaviors and attitudes that are holding back the employee's performance as well. The tasks associated with the everyday managing, training, counseling, and firing are all time -and energy-consuming activities. Sometimes senior manage-ment's desire for a high-performance culture conflicts with an individual manager's desire for job preservation, workload management, hassle avoidance, and conflict avoidance.

What is the right choice? It certainly varies by the company, the industry, the employee's role, the employee, and other factors.

What I always tell my clients is to ask themselves the follow-ing question about an employee: "If the employee in question walked into your office and told you he or she was quitting, would you be happy/relieved or sad about the loss of that person?"

If the answer is that you would be happy and relieved, then *your* answer is simple—you should move the employee through the Absolute Binary counseling process. If you are sad about the prospect of losing the employee, you should ask yourself why. Why are you sad the employee is leaving? It could very well be that even though the employee's performance doesn't meet expectations, the employee performs some tasks that are hard to replicate. If that is the case, then documentation of the tasks and/or cross-training of those tasks is necessary regardless of what you decide to do because the employee may, in fact, quit his or her job. Documentation of the job tasks will then save you time in training his or replacement.

Many years ago, I was acquainted with a man who had bought and sold three staffing companies during his career. As a result, he had a lot of experience hiring and firing, and he had to be extremely effective at hiring people. He taught me his belief that you should "hire slowly and fire quickly." His view was that so few poorly performing employees can be turned around to reach a performance level that is significantly above the standard, it makes no sense to even try to counsel them. I am not so sure.

I have the notion that there are really only three performance categories of employees, regardless of what type of performance appraisal system your company uses:

- Below acceptable

- Acceptable

- Exceptional

In this man's experience, the odds are extremely low that you can bring a person up two notches from below acceptable to exceptional....It can happen, but it is rare. The best you can really hope for is to move an employee up one notch— i.e., to move a poorly performing employee up to acceptable performance or to move an employee with acceptable performance up to a level of exceptional performance. If you accept this idea and if you are really committed to have a high-performance workforce, there is really no point in even attempting to work with the employee who is performing below expectations because the chances of him or her ever becoming exceptional is so low that it isn't worth even attempting it.

This might seem a bit harsh, but for many organizations, the productivity gain that results from having exceptionally performing employees is so great that striving for acceptable isn't worth it. General Electric, under the leadership of Jack Welch, was famous for firing its bottom-performing 10 percent of employees *every single year*. I believe that strategy of *forced ranking* keeps the entire bottom *half* of their employees looking over their shoulder and performing better to keep away from the annual grim reaper. Of course, the top 30 to 50 percent employees are generally that way with little outside motivation, so this policy makes little difference to them. Top performers usually have a lot of internal motivation that keeps them performing at a high level.

While it is tough to argue with this logic, I do believe there are four fundamental flaws in it.

1. First, this idea discounts the cost of hiring and on-boarding new employees. One of the major elements of the cost is that we will have a hole in our organization for some period of time that is going to create a productivity issue. For example, if we have an underperforming employee, wouldn't we rather have a successful intervention that brings his or her productivity up to an acceptable level in the short term than to fire the person and have an unfilled hole in the organization for several months, even if the hiring process *might* yield an exceptional performer? This is not a clear-cut answer, and I can say that in many operational roles, an acceptable performer might be sufficient. A vacancy that remains open while you are waiting to hire and on-board a new employee might be costly to the organization.

2. I think there is a moral and organizational behavior component. At the organizational level, we want to be known as the company that gives people a chance to be successful. On a personal level, as managers and as people, we want things to work out with the underperforming employee. I believe this helps keep our good and even our top performers comfortable because they know they will receive fair treatment if they would ever receive a bad review.

3. Cutting the bottom 10 percent year after year can cause paranoia to develop among your staff because they realize they are ultimately in

competition with each other. They are not just trying to maintain productivity above a certain level, but because all of the incompetents have already been culled, politics can become an increasingly significant factor in who gets fired and who doesn't. Employees who have always been acceptable or even exceptional performers begin to have their confidence and job security undermined. This can lead to a toxic environment. If we believe that innovation really takes place in a collaborative and open environment, a toxically competitive environment can hinder innovation, which is vital to the continued success of any organization. Much has been written about this issue, particularly in its application at Microsoft, where some former employees report a toxic environment brought on by its forced ranking program.

4. Finally, a toxic environment can cause both good and high-performing employees to leave the organization because they fear that they are next whether or not they are even at risk. Not only is this a loss to the company; it can be a significant benefit to the company's competition. The competition has access to high-performing, well trained, experienced people and a better pool of new talent than they would have access to otherwise.

I have always believed that a company can create a system that takes a more holistic management approach to the some of the best ideas of forced ranking. I believe in an approach that captures the high-performance focus while maintaining a healthy, collaborative work environment. In my view, the benefits of forced ranking are that (1) managers are ready, willing, and able to fire underperforming employees and (2) it gives organizations an efficient infrastructure for dealing with their termination of underperformers and hiring and on-boarding of new employees.

With the assumption that fixing underperforming employees is a more efficient and economical approach to management, the next two chapters focus on the theory and practice of managing the underperforming employee to higher perfor-mance.

# Chapter 2

# Managing Employees—Two Theories

It is a funny thing. I have an MBA and have taken my share of management training classes, but when it first came down to actually managing a team, I forgot everything and just worked by the seat of my pants—without much success. It wasn't until months down the road that I started to actually remember and apply a few of the key ideas from those classes into my management job and gain insight and perspective. Management courses present a range of different management and leadership models. All are imperfect, but all can provide insight, and there are certainly others that can apply.

Here are two of the models I have always liked:

- Abraham Maslow's Hierarchy of Needs Model

- Paul Hersey and Ken Blanchard's Situation Leadership II ("SL II") Model

Maslow's model is the classic model of what motivates people in the workplace, and SL II is an interesting model that shows managers how to lead and manage employees based on the employee's level of skill and level of motivation. Combined, these models provide good management information and insight and create a vocabulary for us to use. Let's review these models.

## Maslow's Hierarchy of Needs Model

Abraham Maslow was a psychologist who wrote a seminal paper on human motivation in 1943 published in the academic journal *Psychological Review*. He wrote about how people have a *hierarchy of needs* represented conceptually by a pyramid. The lowest level and broadest foundation of the pyramid is what he considered the most basic—physiological needs like food and shelter. He believed that no one can consider pursuing higher levels of need (represented by the higher levels in the pyramid) *until they have largely satisfied the lower levels of need*. So, for example, people aren't motivated by group belonging until they have satisfied their physiological needs and security needs or if these needs aren't of much importance to them.

I have always found that those employees who tend to be self-motivated performance superstars tend to be at the highest levels of the pyramid. In other words, the best-performing employees tend to be motivated by the characteristics in the top two levels of the pyramid: esteem and self-actualization. Employees with high esteem and self-actualization are either going to work at a high level or they have the confidence to seek opportunities elsewhere if they are not challenged and rewarded.

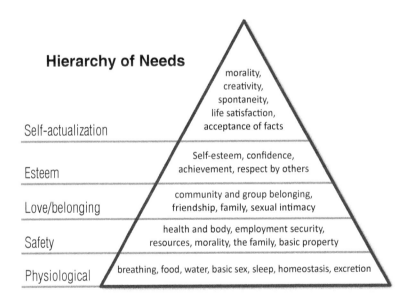

**Hierarchy of Needs**

Self-actualization — morality, creativity, spontaneity, life satisfaction, acceptance of facts

Esteem — Self-esteem, confidence, achievement, respect by others

Love/belonging — community and group belonging, friendship, family, sexual intimacy

Safety — health and body, employment security, resources, morality, the family, basic property

Physiological — breathing, food, water, basic sex, sleep, homeostasis, excretion

You might find it surprising, but your lowest-performing employees are unlikely to be motivated by safety. They tend not to be worried about the economic impact (perhaps irrationally) of their poor performance, or else they would show a much greater commitment. If it isn't motivating them, either it is not important to them or they are in a deep state of denial.

Of course, managing people to reach a high performance level isn't as simple as sending them to a training program. What brings individuals to that level is a combination of their individual internal wiring, their home life (their current situation as well as their experiences growing up), and their work life. Except for the work life, *we are limited in how much influence we can have on employee's motivation.*

This is an important perspective. Some innate factors contribute to employees' motivation and behaviors, and some of them are simply outside the domain of the workplace. As managers, we are limited to what we can possibly influence. We aren't psychotherapists. We can help some employees become motivated, but some we won't be able to help.

I strongly recommend pre-employment testing because it can help identify many of the traits of achievement-oriented and self-motivated people. Employers are looking for those employees who have the personal capability—the potential—to achieve at a high level. Employee testing is not a perfect science, but I believe it increases the chances of making good hiring decisions.

Top-performing employees can be at any level of the pyramid. We aren't necessarily trying to help our employees move to higher levels, but I do believe that if you want an employee to move up to management and executive leadership, he or she needs to move beyond the lower three levels.

The Maslow hierarchy can give managers insight into what motivates employees. It is useful to look for cues that are the hot buttons for motivating employees and to use the hierarchy as a guideline about what other things may motivate them.

We generally think of employees who are motivated by safety as being employees who are also motivated by job security and money, but it is also reasonably common to find those who are motivated by esteem. One of my first jobs as a college graduate was as a technologist for IBM. On our team was a guy who was from a prominent old-money family. Clearly, he wasn't living on his IBM salary alone, but he was an extremely motivated employee who was recognized as one of IBM's most senior technical people. He wasn't motivated by safety or physiological issues; he was highly motivated by the esteem and by the peer and industry recognition his job provided.

A number of Internet resources can help you learn more about Maslow and his needs hierarchy theory, as well as academics who support it and those who criticize it. I have always liked it as a general guideline.

## The Situational Leadership II Model

A second great model and methodology for management style is the Situational Leadership II model, which was first presented by Paul Hersey and Ken Blanchard in their 1969 textbook *Management of Organizational Behavior*. The underlying principle of the idea is that your employees have varying degrees of skill competence and job commitment, with the ideal employee being both *highly competent* and *highly committed*. The least desirable employee is *low on competence* and *low on commitment*. See the following grid:

## Development Levels

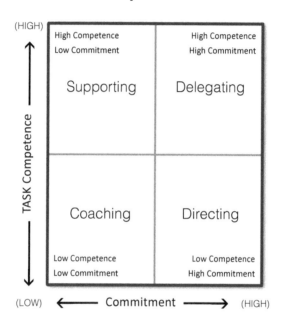

All of your employees fall on the grid somewhere, and there is a management style for employees in each of the quadrants based on how directive vs. how supportive the management style needs to be. The text in the center of each box (Supporting, Delegating, Coaching, and Directing) refers to the recommended management response for the different employee competence and commitment levels.

- **_Low competence, low commitment (It is difficult to fix them.)_**—These employees tend to be our greatest challenge. They have neither the skills nor the commitment to be successful. As managers, we need to find commitment and motivation in these employees. Interestingly, I have found that employees' commitment often increases as their competence increases, so investing in their competence can free the employees up to make a greater commitment. What definitely doesn't work is focusing only on getting employees to commit more without investing in their skill competence. Investing in them shows our commitment to them as tough as it is for us be motivated to train them when they aren't demonstrating commitment I believe it is the only path to turning around these employees.

- **_High competence, low commitment (Motivate them.)_**—These are employees who are skilled but aren't motivated to apply those skills or apply them enthusiastically. These people have the skills to get ahead but don't have the interest or personality to excel. These are employees who need to be shown that making a commitment is worthwhile and can lead to not just continued employment but rewards as well.

- **_Low competence, high commitment (Train them.)_**—These are employees who need training to become more competent in their job responsibilities. With their high commitment, they are likely to be motivated learners. If you give these employees training opportunities such as apprenticeships, and encouragement, you can create top-performing employees. These should be among the easiest to transform their performance.

- **_High competence, high commitment (Recognize and reward them.)_**—Just get out of the way of these top performers! These employees are good at what they do and are committed to the job and the company. These are our ideal employees, and they need little hand holding but do need recognition and support. I have found that many managers don't give enough "love" (attention) to this kind of employee, so they often feel neglected. It is important to think about Maslow with these employees. Many of these employees are motivated by recognition and esteem, so "ignoring" them because they don't "need your help" can often backfire with these employees feeling underappreciated and under recognized.

The concept presented in the Situation Leadership II model is a good way to guide how you can manage employees to improve their performance. Regarding the four quadrants above, it is usually safe to generalize that the employees with high commitment and high skill competence are exceptional performers, and those with low competence and low commitment are below-acceptable performers who would be difficult to turn around. It is in the other two quadrants, with employees of mixed competence and commitment, where we as managers will generally have the greatest impact in raising performance levels.

You can find more information about the Situational Leadership II model on Ken Blanchard's website (http://www.kenblanchard.com), which features references to the available books and training programs on the topic. I encourage you to learn more.

# Chapter 3:

# Managing Employees—Tips on Counseling Employees

First of all, what do I mean by counseling? Counseling is the management process of developing employees through advising, coaching, and guiding in an ongoing cycle of small and large course corrections. The counseling process sets goals and objectives for employees and then manages them to achieve those goals and objectives. For a McDonald's employee, the goals and objectives may be that employees come in on time, be friendly, provide excellent customer service, and master their station, whether it is the order-taking machine or the French fry maker. Another goal may be for the employee to demonstrate leadership within the crew. The manager works with (counsels) the employee to achieve these goals and objectives and to grow to roles of greater responsibility.

When an employee is facing termination for job-performance reasons, he or she is considered to be on a performance improvement plan, which I discussed in Chapter 1. It is a formal counseling plan that a manager uses to try to get an employee's performance up to the acceptable level usually in a prescribed period of time and that is usually ninety days.

The first question we need to ask, before we discuss counseling employees, is this: What is a manager's job? I have seen many managers get a bit confused about this.

A manager's job is not just counseling his or tem team; it is simply this:

> A manager's job is to meet or exceed the goals
> and objectives that have been placed on him/her
> by his/her manager.

Guess what—that is the same "job description" of everyone in the company, except for maybe the CEO, whose goals and objectives are set by the board of directors! The only difference is in *how* you achieve this, as a manager, compared to a non-management, non-supervisory employee. A company accountant's goals and objectives are about mastering professional tasks, sticking to a schedule, etc. A computer programmer's goals and objectives are probably around developing high-quality programs that meet their client's (internal or external) needs. Non-managers achieve or exceed their goals and objectives by mastering the tasks associated with their jobs.

By comparison:

> A manager strives to exceed his/her goals and objectives by maximizing the productivity and creativity of the people in the organization.

For managers to meet or exceed *their* goals and objectives, they have to maximize their team's performance! They need to work through their team to achieve high performance. A manager's success and performance are manifested through the success and performance of their team. Managers can't really exceed their goals and objectives without the team exceeding its goals and objectives unless they do much of the department's work themselves. The counseling process is the process of guiding and coaching your team to achieve maximum performance so that *you* can achieve *your* performance objectives.

If you want to exceed *your* manager's expectation for *you*, your team must, in aggregate, exceed the performance expectations you have for *them*. This is difficult to do if any of your team members are working below what is acceptable and expected. It is also difficult and unfair to expect a team member who is already exceeding expectations to work harder when other team members are not pulling their weight. You cannot accept poor performance from some while demanding great performance from others. This creates a credibility issue and, as a manager, it is vital for you to have the kind of credibility that comes with being impeccably fair to all your team members. It is difficult to manage effectively without credibility. Accepting poor performance from some while demanding high performance from others in an organization isn't fair. It will lead to dissention from your high-performing employees and, ultimately, worse organizational performance.

We can't tolerate poor performance—at least not for very long.

As mentioned in the introduction, I wrote this book for managers in organizations with more than one hundred employees. Nearly all companies of that size have some formal management structures in place, including the following:

- Human resources

- Management guidelines

- Management training

- A formal goal-setting, performance-measurement, and counseling process for employees

- Legal guidelines and procedures in place for counseling and firing people

Any ideas and suggestions provided here should be taken only in the context of existing policies and procedures, particularly the legal guidelines.

I am forever surprised by the difficulty many managers have in managing the underperforming people who work for them. This shouldn't be so hard, right? All we have to do is tell someone what to do and how to do it and then they should just do it, right? I wish it were that simple. This is generally not about employees who don't have the skill to do the work, but simply about employees who don't perform at their potential. Here is what I often hear:

> "John is so frustrating; he never does what I have told him to do. He never follows procedures."

> "I don't understand why Bob can't get nearly as much done as Susan. Doesn't he see how much more Susan gets done? Doesn't he realize that he is recognized as a much poorer performer than anyone in his group?"

If all we needed to do is explain the situation to employees and they would do what we asked, we wouldn't have these problems. Unfortunately, it is way too common that when we either fire an underperforming employee or give him or her a bad review, the employee *is seemingly unaware that there is a critical performance issue.* These employees often respond with surprise and shock. At the same time, to everyone around them, including their peers and other managers, their performance deficiencies are obvious. Aren't we are all constantly amazed that these underperforming employees don't "get" that they are critically substandard performers? Rarely do they see the ax coming for them, and rarely do they act as if the ax is coming for them. What is going on here? How much of this problem lies with the manager and the performance management system, and how much of it lies with the employee?

A number of factors are at play, but I have thought a great deal about the way I have seen people deal with (and rationalize) their underperforming realities. If their friends or family members ask how they are doing at their jobs, they certainly don't tell them that they are being told they are performing below an acceptable level. In their minds--somehow--they aren't. They have rationalized the situation so much that they won't accept the fact that they are underperforming.

I have found that there are seven categories of this type of rationalization:

1. ***Outright denial of the situation***—"My performance is not bad; your measurement of it is flawed."

2. ***Acceptance but...number 1***—"It is true, but I make up for it in other ways, and thus I am valuable to the organization."

3. ***Acceptance but...number 2***—"It is true, but I choose not to try hard because I am above all of this" or "I won't give you my best because you don't deserve it."

**4. Denial by changing the norm**—"You should measure me using different criteria, and in this different measure, I am performing well against what is really important."

**5. Denial by bias ("My manager doesn't like women, minorities, etc.")**—"You can't judge my performance because you are biased against me."

**6. Disqualification of the measurer**—"You are not qualified to measure my performance."

**7. Bad luck**—"You give me the hardest projects, the worst clients, or whatever to work with, so no wonder my performance measures lower than others, and you aren't taking this into consideration."

**8. Acceptance (This one is rare.)**—"It is true. I know I am a poor performer, but I am in denial that my manager realizes it."

And the following are common excuses that underperforming employees give:

- "Yeah, I do less than Susan, Bob, or Fred, but I am the one who plans the Christmas party every year." (Acceptance, but "I make up for it in other ways.")

- "Yeah, I do less than Susan, Bob, or Fred, but they are the exceptions. I am average in the group except for them." (Denial by changing the norm.)

- "Yeah, but I can do so much more. I underperform because I am not challenged or I don't want to be here." ("I am above all this.")

When I work with my clients on this issue, I use the following example as an illustration. Clearly there are people who are above average looking, average looking, and below average looking. Do those who are below average looking admit that? Does anyone *say* their looks are below average? It is doubtful, and it is just as doubtful that people will say they are poor performers in the workplace (or the bedroom, for that matter). Psychologists sometimes call this phenomenon "illusory superiority." It is a phenomenon whereby people tend to overemphasize their positive qualities and underemphasize their negative qualities. In other words, those who are below average would probably say, "I am not the best looking, but I am around average," and that would be good enough for them to avoid dealing with the unpleasant reality of admitting such a thing. This is an example of outright denial.

Telling someone they are below average in looks and getting them to not just *accept* that feedback but to take it as their reality is probably no more difficult than getting someone who is performing at a below-average or unacceptable level to accept that feedback as reality. Owing to the powerful aspect of human nature that is interested in protecting our egos, it isn't easy to accept being less than average in anything. Many, if not most, underperforming people simply do not accept the reality of their performance because of the implication for their ego if they accept that. And if they *are* accepting the reality, how few of those are actually internalizing it to get them out of their comfort zone, to make lasting changes in their performance?

The first way to deal with underperformance is to simply *not allow* denial or rationalization to exist in any form in that person. You need to drive denial and rationalization from the employee's mind. Underperforming employees need to *know*, beyond any doubt, that they are working below an acceptable level and that their employment won't continue at the existing level of performance—in fact, their employment won't continue if they continue to perform anywhere near their current level of performance. This message has to be loud, clear, and beyond any doubt, with no wiggle room. You have to make them believe that you mean business—that you will, beyond any doubt, deliver on this promise. If you do written performance reviews (which I recommend, and they are usually part of larger company's policies and procedures), this performance has to be stated clearly and unambiguously. You also must articulate clearly the definition of the acceptable level of performance. Employees must not be given the opportunity to hide their performance or to hide behind their excuses for their performance. They have to accept it.

In general, interpersonal communication is a fundamentally flawed process. Throughout our lives, we think we are saying one thing, but the person we are talking to hears or interprets something different. This is no different in the communication process associated with giving feedback to employees or guiding them during the goal-setting and counseling process. You will inevitably have the experience in which you believe an employee's performance is at one level and the employee believes it is something else entirely. We all have listening filters that our emotions create. When people are told that they are underperforming, it eats at their essential ego and evokes an emotional, protective response. You have to be aware of this and try not to let it happen. A good way to understand what the employee has heard is to ask him or her to repeat a summary back to you of the things he or she will do to meet expectations.

Years ago, I was giving a review to an underperforming woman who worked for me. In her review, I told her that her performance was below where it needed to be and suggested where it could be. She disagreed with me, and she pointed out that my assessment was largely subjective and not based on her actual quantifiable performance. Many times, a person's job performance can be assessed only on subjective terms and regardless of how measureable a person's performance may seem to be. Frequently, extenuating circumstances exist, and it is up to the manager to either take them into consideration or disregard them.

---

I told her, "My perception is your reality." In other words, I didn't care if she believed that my assessment of her performance was subjective and incorrect—she had to live in that world. My perception was going to influence her destiny, determine her promotions, influence whether or not she would get laid off or fired, and result in a whole host of other realities in her life. If my perception was incorrect, then she needed to influence that perception to improve her performance assessment.

As managers, we need to be open to the idea that our perceptions may need to be revised. To her credit, she did change my perception. She was, in fact, performing better than I had perceived, and because she was something of an introvert, I didn't really know the extent of her performance. My lesson learned: Don't be biased when an employee is something of an introvert. Her lesson learned: Managing the perceptions of your performance is as important as the performance itself. Life is a journey.

When you are able to make someone accept that they are underperforming, you are piercing the protective bubble they live in. This bubble protects their ego and has been letting them believe that they are good at what they do, which for many people is a key part of who they are and their ego. A message that pierces this bubble can be difficult for people to accept and easy for them to deny to protect their ego. *To break through this bubble, employees need to hear the message several times, at least*—not just during the final session when they are being fired.

We need to break that protective bubble, but we really need to leave some of their ego intact or they won't believe they can improve. You don't need to be heartless about it, and really crushing someone can be counterproductive because our first objective is always to get people to improve their performance.

Destroying people's egos isn't going to be the key to getting them to turn around their performance. Remember, you don't really *prefer* to fire them! If you break their protective bubble gently and make them face *their* reality (notice I wrote "*their* reality," not "*the* reality") of their job situation, the less trauma will be present in this entire process, including when and if the person is fired later. Too much trauma during the counseling process will make it difficult to get employees to see things clearly and will make it difficult to get them to admit to you and themselves that their performance has, indeed, been below acceptable. Most importantly, a traumatic experience will leave the employee with too little ego intact to allow him or her to *risk* trying harder to improve performance.

Asking people to improve their performance requires them to risk their already damaged egos in the process of trying to change their performance. If they take that risk and still fail, it could be really painful for them. We need to encourage our employees to be willing to take that risk by assuring them that they can be successful and letting them know that we are there to help them be successful.

Here are some specific things to keep in mind when you are counseling an underperforming employee:

- You must make underperforming employees understand that their performance is considered below acceptable and that they are facing termination if they do not raise their performance to the level specified by the performance improvement plan.

- You must explain the situation so that employees understand what they need to do. For example, they might need to change their productivity, their output, or a personality trait; show leadership; or improve work quality. To the degree possible, you need to explain and define measures of success so that both you and the employee are in complete agreement about what needs to get done.

- Employees must have absolute clarity and agreement with you that they understand where they are, what needs to change, and the specific ramifications for not achieving the necessary changes in performance, in the time frame you stipulate. You have to try your best to make sure they are not rationalizing away your comments about their performance.

- You must be willing to provide support and guidance so that employees can make these changes. You need to assure employees that you are there to help them be successful.

- The ninety-day performance improvement plan I discussed in Chapter 1 must be stated in very clear terms so that the decision whether to keep them or fire them comes down to something like a checklist—no tie scores, no exceeding one objective to make up for coming up short on another. You need to make and follow a list of yes/no questions that *all* require "yes" answers or else the employee is out the door. This list must be very clear to the employee, and the measures must be as objective as possible.

- You should be open to discussing the role of perceptions and how your perceptions are the employee's reality. If the employee believes your perceptions are not valid, you should challenge him or her to change those perceptions.

The most important point is that it is vital for the employee to understand and understand completely that he or she is facing termination. This is important for two key reasons:

1. If anything is going to help motivate the employee to change behavior, it is the fact that he or she is facing termination. *Employees need to know that*

*being terminated is really a decision that is in their hands.* They need to be clear that termination is a potential reality. Often, that is the only thing that can cut through the cloud of their internal rationalization and invalid self-perception.

2. If you end up having to terminate the employee, the fact that you have set an expectation and that you have ensured that the employee understands what actions or inactions will lead to the termination will make the termination discussion simple and straightforward. There will be no surprises, and it will be a lot less traumatic for you, the manager. The last thing you want the employee to say to you when you terminate them is that this is coming as a surprise.

Firing an employee is the last step when, despite your most sincere efforts, you are unable to improve an employee's performance to an acceptable level. As a manager, I cannot help but consider having to fire someone something of a personal performance failure, to some degree. It means that I either hired an incompetent employee or I was unable to get the employee to perform at an acceptable level. In either case, I wish I could have done better and had a successful outcome but, of course, not all employees are fixable! People come to their jobs with all sorts of issues that hold back their performance—from a lack of desire to be in the job to things happening in their lives outside of work to psychological issues.

Ultimately, using the approach I have outlined gives employees every opportunity to be successful, but poor performers fire themselves. There is no reason for us to feel guilty (or be made to feel guilty) over this outcome.

# Chapter 4:

# Your Mindset when Firing Someone

Unless you are a cold-hearted person, firing someone is going to be an unpleasant or even traumatic event for you, for a number of reasons. The fear of that trauma is the *anxiety* we feel about having this tough conversation. "Anxiety" is defined as the fear of imminent pain or discomfort. Let's go through the causes of this anxiety so that you have a better understanding of the dynamics at play and what mindset you must overcome to fire someone successfully and smoothly.

Here are four primary reasons that firing someone causes anxiety:

1. By firing someone, you are inevitably creating hardship in his or her life. The person will have to go home and tell his or her spouse, family, and

friends of the situation—or lie about it. Plus, he or she might very well suffer financial hardship as a result of being fired. It isn't easy to put forces in motion that will create hardship for others, and it is natural that we would be reluctant to do it.

2. The employee may have an emotional or violent response, possibly directed at you, when you fire him or her. Some people cry, and others scream and yell because they feel that you have served them an injustice, and they will direct that anger at you. To emotionally protect yourself, it is important that you have done what we have talked about here to help the employee succeed and that you have made yourself really clear to the employee about the current situation. If you do so and you still have to fire the person, it is less likely that he or she is going to be upset because you have the moral high ground in the situation. If the person is upset, he or she will be less likely to focus that energy on you because they know or suspected it could be coming and why. The techniques discussed in this book will minimize the chance of any conflict. Few people like conflict, but properly preparing the person to be fired and communicating the message well will dramatically reduce the chances of an emotional eruption.

3. The third cause of anxiety that I have found is that the manager who has made the separation decision and has to have the talk with the employee is afraid that the employee will talk him or her out of the decision during the exit meeting. Managers are sometimes afraid that they may be wrong in their own assessment and that their process of deciding that the employee should be fired is in error. They are afraid they will be convinced not to complete the separation. They are afraid that the employee will use emotional blackmail—in other words, "seduce" or "guilt-lobby" the manager (make the manager feel guilty)—into keeping him or her on. I have found that this lack of confidence in the termination decision is the result of a poorly conceived performance plan. If the performance plan really identifies the key criteria for job success and has clear measures there should be little room for doubt in the manager's mind.

4. A less frequent reason that firing someone causes anxiety among managers is that some managers consider it to be recognition of a failure on *their* part. This is because, as managers, it is frustrating that despite our best efforts, we couldn't get the desired performance out of someone. It is

inevitable that you have to invest a lot of time and emotional energy into all your employees and their development—particularly those who need a lot of counseling and direct management. It is frustrating that all that of your investment has gone for naught—you are giving up on them. Having to terminate someone also can be seen as a failure by the firing manager's management. This is an issue I have personally experienced.

Many years ago, I was running a company in New York City. I had a receptionist who was the bane of my existence. I simply couldn't get her to answer the phone with the professionalism I wanted our company to project. I would frequently call in on the main number to check up on how she was answering the phone. She continued to answer the phone the way she wanted to, not the way I wanted her to. I ended up firing her. I considered myself to be a good manager, but I couldn't get our receptionist to do the job the way I wanted her to. I was supposed to be able to manage a sales team, a finance team, an HR team, and an engineering team, but I couldn't even get our receptionist to do her job right! It was quite frustrating, and I internalized it to the point that I am still talking about it more than fifteen years later!

Ensuring that the employee truly understands the situation, his or her performance, its measures, what he or she needs to do, and the deadline for change will dramatically reduce the anxiety and trauma associated with firing an employee.

An employee who has been effectively counseled on his or her performance either knows that he or she is close to getting fired or lives in a world of denial about the situation. If employees have been counseled thoroughly, they will have no place to hide from the reality of the situation. They will see that they have either made a conscious choice not to do the things they need to do to be successful, or they don't have the skills to be successful.

In any of the following cases, you are not responsible; you have done everything a manager can do:

1. If you have communicated the employee's performance issues, and he or she refuses to accept it, you are not responsible.

2. If the employee refuses to do the work as directed, you are not responsible.

3. If the employee doesn't have the skills needed to do the job, then he or she misrepresented skills or abilities he or she had when hired, or things changed and the job now requires different skills. If the employee has not sought out the needed skills, you are not responsible.

4. If the employee has a psychological issue that is keeping him or her from performing, you are not responsible.

5. If situations in the employee's life outside of work are affecting his or her productivity, you are not responsible. This, too, isn't your issue.

If you are doing what you should be doing in the counseling process, your team will be divided into two groups: the performers who are confident in their job security and the nonperformers who have received clear communication about the situation they are facing if they do not join the ranks of the performers.

Here are several perspectives that are important for you to keep in mind if you are hesitant to go through with a termination:

1. ***The person being fired has chosen the behavior or performance level that has led to this situation, in the majority of cases.***
   Inaction is a conscious choice. The employee probably had the potential to do more but chose not to. It is not your responsibility if the person won't help himself or herself, and you should not feel bad if you then choose to "make them available to industry."

**2. The person being fired is being fired because he or she is incapable of doing the job for one reason or another, in the rest of the cases.**

You gave the person an opportunity to "rise to the occasion," but he or she either couldn't or wouldn't make the jump. You gave the employee a chance, so how can this be your responsibility? It isn't your responsibility if the person doesn't have the skills to be successful and can't, won't, or doesn't learn them. You are not running a charity; you are running a business.

**3. Underperformers are costing you and/or your company money.**

Being an owner or manager of an entrepreneurial company is a great teacher. Underperforming people cost you or your company money every day. They dilute the effectiveness of your team. They are a weak link that causes a department's performance to suffer or causes the other people in the department, including you, to work harder to carry the underperformer's burden. You are responsible to *your* management to spend company money efficiently, and spending money on an underperformer violates *your* responsibility to the company.

**4. They are setting a bad example for the rest of your team.**

The weakest link in the department or your company sets an example for your team of what is considered minimally acceptable behavior. This is a very important point. Because you are letting them behave and perform this way and are not firing them, it must be an acceptable level of performance. You are declaring what acceptable performance is by your actions, which always speak louder than your words. Firing the weakest link sends a message to your team that they had better not be the weakest link! I have generally noted a sense of relief among the remaining employees when the weakest link is fired because it means that the entire team has been strengthened. Everyone works harder and is more focused, and you are seen as decisive and fair.

**5. Not firing or delaying the firing of the underperforming employee may be holding you back professionally.**

*Your* management sees what is going on. Do you want your management to think that you are someone who can't make tough decisions? Do you want your management to think you are not performance-oriented because you aren't doing something to improve your team's performance? I am certain that you don't.

**6. Delaying the inevitable is holding back underperforming employees from finding what they should be doing for a living.**

The sooner they get on with their lives, the sooner they can start being on the right path for them to the right job and career, which may be a path of self-discovery for them. They may just need to be fired to get a clear message about their need for a new career direction. They need to either figure out what they should be doing or start doing it!

**7. The employee may be unhappy with his or her job and just doesn't have the guts to quit.**

When people hate their job and it *shows*, it seeds bad *esprit de corps* in the organization. Ending this negative spiral will make both of you happier in the long run.

Employees are either *capable* of doing the work satisfactorily or they aren't. If they aren't capable, all the coaching and counseling in the world isn't going make them capable. If they are capable of doing the work but are unwilling to do so, it is probably for one of three reasons. One reason is that he or she is unhappy in the job and is acting out—like a child. The second reason is that the person may want to get fired and collect unemployment insurance or some kind of company separation package. The third reason is that the person is clueless about how to function in the work world. I have come across a lot of employees (typically younger employees because most older employees have figured it out by now or are out of the workforce) who have been coddled their whole lives. People rarely demanded anything of them, and they were never held accountable for their performance. The fastest and possibly the most effective way, short of joining the Marine Corps, for them to get a clue is for them to experience a traumatic event like being fired. They have been coddled for too long. It may surprise you, but employees you fire may very well be grateful to you down the road. Many of the employees I have fired have, years later, told me that they are grateful for the wake-up call the termination provided.

When you fire someone, you have a choice between telling the employee the hard truth about his or her performance or candy-coating it and letting them blame bad luck, their circumstances, or other outside factors for losing their job. If you candy-coat the situation, you are ultimately doing them a great disservice. Employee who are being fired for performance reasons need to either change themselves or change their career/profession to be happy and successful. Candy-coating the issue just allows the employee to avoid the introspection and the emotional jolt necessary to make these sometimes fundamental changes. You owe it to employees to be honest and direct. Anything else is just setting them up for failure in their next job.

Remember, those employees you keep on staff who perform at a below-acceptable level set the bar of what is *acceptable* behavior on your team. If you put up with bad performance, bad work habits, and bad energy from an employee, the other employees will know that they can drop their performance that low and get away with it.

In contrast, if you have no patience for poor performance, everyone will know they need to perform well, so it will pull everyone's performance up. Everyone in your organization knows who the poor performers are. Your top performers are possibly more frustrated than you are with the underper-formers and with the fact that you are keeping them around. This has a seriously detrimental effect on your whole team's performance and spirit.

# Chapter 5:

# The Script for Firing Employees without Trauma

The key to making the termination process smooth and trauma-free, regardless of the method you use, is planning. Part of planning is being prepared for the difficult conversations that surround the termination process. The script in this chapter will arm you with specific language to use in communicating the termination decision to employees. Having a script will help you avoid personalizing the communication, and it will help you terminate employees in a consistent manner.

The best type of termination for all concerned is the quickest and cleanest one, especially when the employee has the potential to access sensitive information, can copy contacts, or damage strategic information. You need to plan so that there are no major questions from the employee you don't have an answer for and so that the employee cannot derail the process.

Each company has its own procedural steps that its leadership will want done, but the following are three details to plan for.

## Avoiding the "End Around"

When firing an employee, he or she may look for a way to halt or delay the process. Here are two possibilities:

- **By the employee wanting to go to your senior management**—The employee may look to speak to a senior company executive who can either find him or her another position in the company or make you give the employee another chance. It is imperative that you have at least your manager and, if possible, your manager's manager supporting your decision and your authority to make the decision. The last thing you want is to have your authority undermined. When you have the termination meeting with the employee, you want to be clear that you have the authority and support of senior management.

- **By the employee wanting to go to your Human Resources department**—There may be a reason known only to Human Resources why this person can't be fired or can't be fired at this time. I know of a situation in which HR delayed a termination process because they felt that they had fired too many of that protected employee class in recent weeks, and they felt it might expose them to bad publicity or even legal action. This is an unfortunate reality of contemporary times.

## Asset Protection

When an employee leaves, whether the decision is self-initiated or company-initiated, make sure company assets (including data) are protected.

- **Change passwords**—Change passwords immediately. If the employee tells you that he or she has some personal files on their computer to retrieve, tell the person to request them from the company in writing and have someone from IT or your staff send them the files after ensuring that they don't have any competitive or other sensitive information in them.

- **Revoke access to data, systems, and physical access**—From the moment you start the termination meeting and say the magic words "You are fired" (or something like that), the person you are terminating is no long an employee of the company. He or she should not have access to any part of the company without escort. You do not want this person wandering around complaining about how he or she was treated, sowing dissent, destroying assets, helping themselves to office supplies or distracting the other employees.

- **Secure laptops, cell phones, and other company property**—If the employee doesn't have a company asset with him or her when you have the termination meeting, find out if it is legal to hold back severance until the assets are returned.

- **Get the company car back**—If the employee has a company car, make sure you can immediately take it from the employee and make arrangements with a taxi or car service to get him or her home safely. You may want to call the car service once the employee starts to clear out his or her desk and office so that the employee doesn't linger. You want the employee out!

- **Revoke credit and gas cards**—I screwed up on this once. We fired someone and forgot to cancel his company credit card. Then he went out and bought a few thousand dollars' worth of consumer electronics toys. By the time I found out, I had already given him his severance pay. We ended up taking him to small-claims court to collect on the money owed but were ultimately unsuccessful in collecting the judgment. Revoke the company credit card!

When I was a manager, I coordinated with HR and IT when I was firing an employee so that the moment the employee walked into my office, I would send a text to IT and HR to implement the asset-protection procedure immediately so that by the time I was done with the "big talk," everything would be secure.

## Administration

The following are some other preparations you need to make in advance of the termination meeting.

- **Coordinate with HR**—If you are going to have someone from HR in the room, make sure the meeting is scheduled. It is often advisable to have a witness in the room when you terminate an employee.

- **Understand the company severance policy and how it will apply**—Many companies have some flexibility in their severance policy. Make sure you know what the policy is and how it will be applied in each case. You want to be able to answer the employee's questions about severance and continuation of benefits (e.g., when health care coverage will end).

- **Understand COBRA and what the employee needs to do**—COBRA is the set of regulations that allow terminated employees to continue their health care benefits if they decide to pay for them on their own. They will likely have questions about it. If your company doesn't have an information packet about COBRA, encourage your HR department to prepare one for you.

- **Prepare corporate communications**—How will you announce to the rest of the company, customers, vendors, and business partners that the employee is being terminated? With customer-facing employees, it often makes sense for a person (or persons) with authority to call key customers and people whom the employee had important business relationships with to notify them about the termination. If you are firing someone in a supervisory position, it might make sense for you or the employee's replacement or acting replacement (or you) to call a meeting of the staff who had reported to that person to explain the situation and assure them of positive changes that will result.

- **Have the employee sign a confidentiality agreement**—Even if you have a company policy that requires new employees to sign confidentiality, non-compete (can't work for a competitor), or non-solicitation (can't solicit existing clients or employees) agreements, it is often a good idea to have the employee sign new ones. I recommend to my clients that they tell the employee that paying them severance beyond a minimum amount is contingent on their signing new agreements. If nothing else, it serves as a reminder of the agreements they signed in the past that are still applicable.

## Two Ways to Fire People

There are fundamentally only two ways to fire people: the "storytelling" method, which I don't recommend, and the "top–down" method, which I strongly advocate.

### *The Storytelling Method*

The storytelling method turns firing someone into a story that is told to the employee. It often goes like this: "Once upon a time, we hired you with great optimism, then something happened, then something else happened, then we weren't happy with your performance. We tried to make you better, and it hasn't produced the results we wanted, so now you are fired."

The storytelling, or timeline, method takes employees along a timeline that brings them to the situation that they are in today (being fired). I consider this to be something of a bottom-up approach that builds a story or argument over a timeline, with the conclusion that the employee is being fired.

The advantage of this communication method is that it takes the employee through the process so that he or she has some additional understanding of how you reached your decision. The disadvantages, on the other hand, are more numerous and significant.

The main disadvantage of this system is that it simply gives the employee too much opportunity to disagree with the facts as you present them. When you say something like, "...and two years ago, we gave you a bad review because you failed to deliver the XYZ project on time," the employee can respond by saying, "Yeah, but you know the reason I didn't get that done was because I didn't get sufficient support from IT...." At this point, the discussion falls into a discussion about what happened two years ago and how he or she should have handled it, company politics, how IT is always making life difficult, and a million other things. By taking the employee through the history in this way, he or she mentally participates in the story you have outlined.

This type of interruption creates two problems. First, it transforms the conversation from a termination discussion to a discussion about everything *but* the termination. Second, it slows the momentum of the termination discussion. After being distracted several times, by the time you reach the culmination of where you are going—to tell the employee he or she is fired—you have given the employee a tremendous amount of time and energy to discuss myriad other issues. You have set the stage for a *dialogue* about those issues, allowing the employee to rehash why IT or politics or something else is the root cause of his or her demise. This is simply not helpful to you or the employee.

The worst part of the storytelling or timeline approach is that the dialogue gives the employee an opportunity to try to coerce you into believing that there may be a question about the rigor of your decision-making process or your data. You *knew* during the previous weeks or months of working with this employee that he or she was underperforming and not improving in terms of performance, but right now, after all the dialogue that has gone on, you are wondering about whether IT made this employee look bad, whether he or she is the victim of company politics, and whether you are being fair. The reality is that ninety-nine times out of a hundred, these are all smokescreens. These tactics create anxiety in the firing manager.

Years ago, I was driving around Germany in a rental car (Hertz rented Porches at the time), and the local German police pulled me over for speeding. (The irony was that I was pulled over for driving the equivalent of 40 mph in a 30-mph zone minutes after driving faster than 120 mph on the Autobahn). I figured I could use my poor German to my advantage. I took out a map and asked the officer for directions back to my hotel. Whenever he said anything about my speed or looked at my license or car registration, I went back to asking him more questions about how to get to Berlin and which roads were best. Ultimately, I got the policeman so involved in talking to me about how to get to Berlin that I was sent on my way without a ticket—and with a smile on my face.

Understand that for someone being fired, one of the best strategies is to divert the conversation to everything *but* the fact that he or she is being fired. It is likely that your employees will employ this technique if you use a timeline approach.

You are exposing your methodology of how you arrived at the decision, and they will attack the methodology. You are exposing the data you are applying to the methodology, and they will attack the data. They also will attack your management abilities—all for their own self-preservation and anger venting.

The employee wants to debate you, so the best way to fire an employee is to inform him or her of a decision that has already been made and is not subject to debate or even discussion. You want to present to the person that he or she is terminated and that it is a *fait accompli*. I do this with what I call the top–down method.

### The Top–Down Method

Using the top–down approach, someone informs the employee of the decision to terminate, and then the manager immediately begins to act in a post-termination mode. No excuses are given because if the counseling sessions leading up to this point have been effective, the employee will know why he or she is being terminated. The employee was told what he or she needed to do but has not done it. The termination meeting is just a confirmation of what the employee has been expecting. It isn't a surprise. There is no room for debate.

A detailed discussion of a termination script is presented later in this chapter, but here is the basic format:

> "Bob, today will be your last day with us. Susan (Bob's boss's boss or some other senior executive in the command chain) is on board with this. You and I have talked about this, and we both know that this isn't working out."

> "The company has approved the following severance package…. Here are your forms for COBRA. If you have any questions about severance or COBRA, please contact Mike in Human Resources. He is on board with this and knows that you might call him. Remember the confidentiality and other agreements you signed and your continuing responsibilities. The agreements run for several years (or whatever) from your termination date, and the company will enforce those agreements vigorously. Here is a box for your personal belongings. We would like you to gather up your things and be on your way."

*That is it! Say nothing more. Don't even ask if the employee has any questions.* I discuss how to handle questions below if they ask questions. When the employee gets up to collect his or her belongings, there might be a long pause. Just say this:

"I have enjoyed working with you, and I am truly sorry things didn't work out. Let me know if I can be of assistance in your job search. I wish you the best of luck."

Done. Elapsed time should be about three minutes.

Now let's break down the steps in detail. The following script will guide you through the termination:

### Step 1—Communicate the decision:

*"Bob, today will be your last day with us. Susan is on board with this."* The decision is presented as a *fait accompli*, and senior management is aware of the decision. You have discussed this with senior management, and they approve or support this decision. The decision is made. There is no point in the employee going over your head to senior management for one more chance. These opening sentences are loud and clear—you and the employee are not there to discuss this; you are there to communicate a management-supported decision to the employee. You are not giving him or her an opportunity to participate in the process. This is not a debate; it is a unilateral communication. You are communicating the person's new reality.

### Step 2—Connect it to previous conversations:

*"You and I have talked about this, and we both know this isn't working out."* The employee has to realize that you weren't making an empty promise. At this point, employees realize that their rationalization of their performance was flawed.

### Step 3—Discuss pay and paperwork:

*"The company has approved the following severance package.... Here are your COBRA forms. If you have any questions about severance or COBRA, please contact Mike in Human Resources."*

And now the employee starts to think: *All the details are in place. Other people in other departments are involved, and that means that meetings and calls have taken place about this. This decision has been implemented throughout the company's administration systems; it is really a done deal. I can't undo all of this. I can't convince my manager to give me another chance now; he would never reverse all these things. This decision doesn't just exist in my department, but it has been implemented companywide. It is a decision that can't be undone.*

### Step 4—Remind the employee about the agreements: *"Remember the confidentiality and other agreements you signed and your continuing responsibilities. They run for several*

FIX THEM OR FIRE THEM

*years (or whatever) from your termination date,
and the company will vigorously enforce those
agreements."*

Employees sign a lot of documents their first day on the job, and if it is your company's policy that employees sign confidentiality, non-compete, and/or non-solicitation agreements, you need, at a minimum, to remind them that they signed them and that they will be enforced. As discussed earlier, I always encourage my clients to have terminated employees sign new agreements so that they are fresh in their minds and so that if it needs to be enforced, we are enforcing recently signed agreements rather than documents that are years old. These are not the same documents that new employees sign. The language should be specific to former employees and their continuing responsibilities as a former employee.

**Step 5—Ask him or her to gather personal belongings:** *"Here is a box for your personal belongings. We would like you to gather up your things and be on your way."*

The employee should realize that there is nothing to talk about and no room for discussion. Taking the box should act as a cue for him or her to get up and move to the door. This usually works best when someone from HR is standing in your office or right outside to walk the person to his or her desk or office. Because the person is no longer an employee, he or she shouldn't be allowed to walk unescorted around the building, venting anger and sowing seeds of dissent. You want the person gone.

> **Step 6—Say goodbye:** *"I have enjoyed working with you, and I am truly sorry things didn't work out. Let me know if I can be of assistance in your job search. I wish you the best of luck."* Of course you are sorry things didn't work out; you are now facing a great deal of effort in having to find a replacement. Nothing would have been better if things had worked out. While this approach is direct, it isn't heartless. There is no reason to be mean about this. It is also important at this step not to apologize for firing the person. It is OK to apologize generally that things didn't work out, but don't apologize for the termination. It is important to keep reminding yourself that the employee has chosen this situation. He or she had an opportunity to avoid this but chose not to. Apologizing for firing him or her is just going to be interpreted as your being unsure of yourself or as a sign of weakness. Neither of these is helpful for the employee or you.

You will probably be feeling bad and will want to try to soften the blow. Actively resist the urge to start to explain things to make you or the terminated employee feel better because this will put you in an unscripted situation, and you could well say things that could come back to haunt you. Again, keep thinking of the question, "If the employee was not so bad, then why did you fire him or her?" Remember their performance plan and that the employee did not satisfy the performance measures on it.

After the person leaves, close your office door and take a deep breath. *It is done.*

Let's discuss what kind of questions employees tend to ask (when they ask any at all) or comments they often make during the process and appropriate responses. It is important to remember that every answer you give shouldn't slow down the process of getting the person out of the building.

- **Question:** I want to talk to Susan (or another senior manager) about this.

  **Answer:** Feel free to give Susan a call when you get home or later this week, but she supports this decision and agrees that today will be your last day.

- **Question:** I am entitled to more severance than this.

  **Answer:** Contact HR when you get home or tomorrow to discuss how it was calculated. If there are any discrepancies, we will make an adjustment—no problem. Alternatively, send me an e-mail, and I will forward it to HR and whomever else to review your severance calculation.

- **Question:** Is this decision made, or is this something we can discuss?

  **Answer:** The decision has been made that today will be your last day and is supported by senior management.

- **Question:** I really feel that I wasn't treated fairly in this process.

  **Answer:** I am sorry you feel that way, but the decision stands that today will be your last day, and the decision is supported by senior management.

- **Question:** Is there anything I can do to get another chance?

  **Answer:** No. The decision has been made that today will be your last day.

- **Question:** How (or what) will I tell my significant other?

  **Answer:** Just tell him/her; he/she will understand. You must have seen this coming in our counseling sessions; this can't be a total surprise to you.

- **Question:** What am I going to do? I can't afford to be out of work.

  **Answer:** I don't mean to be harsh about this, but you have to be responsible for yourself. You certainly never treated this job as something that was so important to you or you wouldn't be finding yourself in this situation. In fairness to all employees and the owners, this company can't afford to have underperformers on the payroll. You know that.

- **Question:** I don't understand how this could be happening.

    **Answer:** Don't you recall that we have had several meetings in which we talked about your performance being below what is acceptable? Do you remember that? Do you remember how I told you that if your performance didn't improve to the performance level we discussed, we would have to let you go? Well, here we are.

- **Question:** Why? How did this happen?

    **Answer:** I just don't think you are happy here, and it shows in your performance. When you find a place where you are happy, I am sure your performance will be great.

Notice how in most answers, I keep going back to "the decision has been made that today will be your last day." It is vital that each answer is impersonal. For example, saying "I have decided that today will be your last day" can create a *personal* tension between you and the employee. It creates the impression that you are personally making the decision (even if it is true). Making it a simple statement of fact reduces the anger and emotion. It makes it seem like a company decision that you are delivering that is not likely to be changed or disputed. It also gives the statement a greater sense of finality.

Also notice how I make employees participants in the situation when I can. They are ultimately responsible for the situation they find themselves in and need to be reminded of that. They knew, or certainly should have known, that this was coming. This goes back to the importance of clear communication during the counseling process. Employees really need to know that their performance needs to improve or they will be fired. You as a manager need to make sure you develop personal credibility so that when you make those kinds of statements, your employees realize they aren't empty words.

# Epilogue: Now What?

In today's increasingly competitive business world, every organization has to drive itself to higher and higher performance levels just to stay in the game. This drive for greater performance levels affects every employee such that there simply isn't any room for underperforming employees *or* managers. As managers we need to be relentless in our managerial efforts and relentless in the continuous improvement of our skills.

Having tough conversations and counseling sessions with employees about unacceptable performance or having to fire the employees are never going to be easy or pleasant. Preparation and even role play with colleagues are going to be the keys to making it easier and minimizing the unpleasantness. Prepare yourself with the material in the book before you jump into these situations. Like any other skill, counseling and firing underperforming employees get easier with practice. Review this material and use it.

I have set up a forum on my website (http://fixthemorfirethem.com) as a place to ask questions about and discuss the Absolute Binary Performance Plan and the top–down method of firing employees. If you have any questions or would like to see others' questions and answers, please feel free to sign up and leave your questions there. I will also publish other resources and templates there as they become available.

CPSIA information can be obtained
at www.ICGtesting.com
Printed in the USA
LVHW021533140421
684521LV00010B/1049